People in the Community

Police Officers

Diyan Leake

www.raintreepublishers.co.uk
Visit our website to find out
more information about
Raintree books.

To order:
☎ Phone 0845 6044371
🖷 Fax +44 (0) 1865 312263
🖳 Email myorders@raintreepublishers.co.uk

Customers from outside the UK please telephone +44 1865 312262

Raintree is an imprint of Capstone Global Library Limited, a company
incorporated in England and Wales having its registered office at 7 Pilgrim Street,
London, EC4V 6LB – Registered company number: 6695582

Editorial: Diyan Leake and Catherine Clarke
Design: Joanna Hinton-Malivoire and Steve Mead
Picture research: Tracy Cummins and Heather Maudlin
Production: Alison Parsons
Origination: Chroma Graphics (Overseas) Pte Ltd
Printed and bound in China by South China Printing Company Ltd

ISBN 978 0 431 19245 1 (hardback)
12 11 10 09 08
10 9 8 7 6 5 4 3 2 1

ISBN 978 1 406 25467 9 (paperback)
13 12
10 9 8 7 6 5 4

British Library Cataloguing in Publication Data
Leake, Diyan
Police officers. - (People in the community)

A full catalogue record for this book is available from the
British Library.

Acknowledgments
The publishers would like to thank the following for permission to reproduce
photographs:
©Age Fotostock pp. **6** (UpperCut Images), **8** (Jeremy Woodhouse), **11**
(Anton J. Geisser), **12** (Kevin O'Hara), **14** (Ben Walsh), **16** (Gonzalo
Azumendi), **21** (Jeff Greenberg), **22 (bottom)** (Kevin O'Hara); ©Alamy
pp. **9** (Vehbi Koca), **15** (Mike Abrahams), **22 (middle)** (Mike Abrahams);
©AP Photo (Remy de la Mauviniere) p. **19**; ©Corbis (Bojan Brecelj) p.
13; ©DigitalRailroad.net (GalileoPix/Oote Boe) p. **7**; ©Getty Images pp.
4 (Gavin Hellier), **5** (Andrew Holt), **10** (Jeff Brass), **20** (Yoshikazu Tsuno/
AFP), **22 (top)** (Gavin Hellier); ©Reuters (Rafiqur Rahman/Landov) p. **18**;
©Shutterstock (Pres Panayotov) p. **17**.

Front cover photograph of a police officer on horseback reproduced with
permission of ©Reuters (Ian Hodgson). Back cover photograph reproduced
with permission of ©Age Fotostock (Jeremy Woodhouse).

Every effort has been made to contact copyright holders of any material
reproduced in this book. Any omissions will be rectified in subsequent print-
ings if notice is given to the publisher.

Contents

Communities

People live in communities. They live near each other and help each other.

People work together in a
community.

Police officers in the community

Police officers work in communities.

Police officers help people to stay safe.

What police officers do

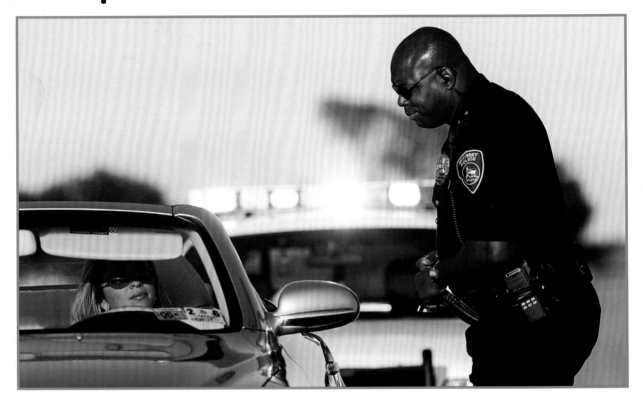

Police officers help to keep traffic safe.

Police officers help people who
are lost.

Police officers help if there is
an accident.

Police officers stop people if they have done something wrong.

What police officers wear

Police officers wear uniforms.

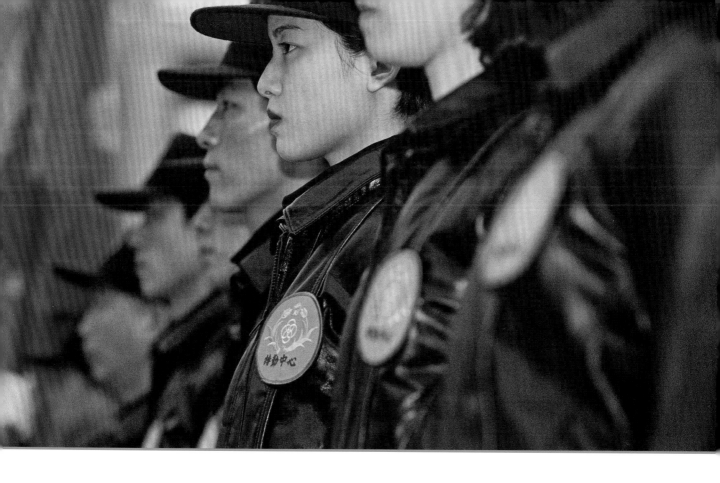

Police officers wear badges.

Where police officers work

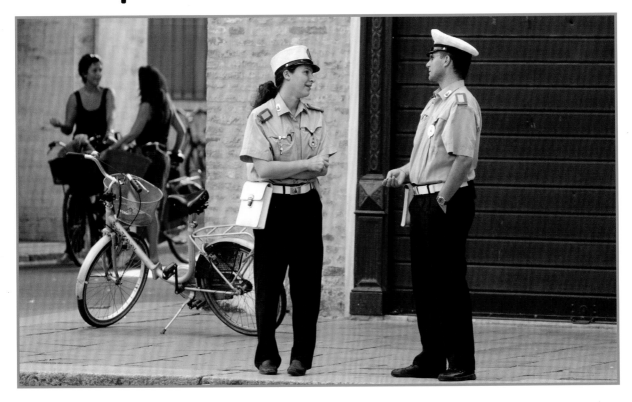

Police officers work in towns and in the countryside.

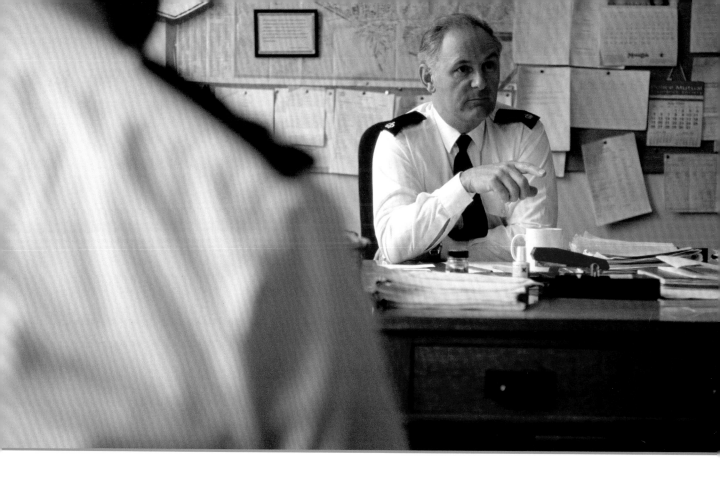

Police officers work in police stations.

Police officers on the go

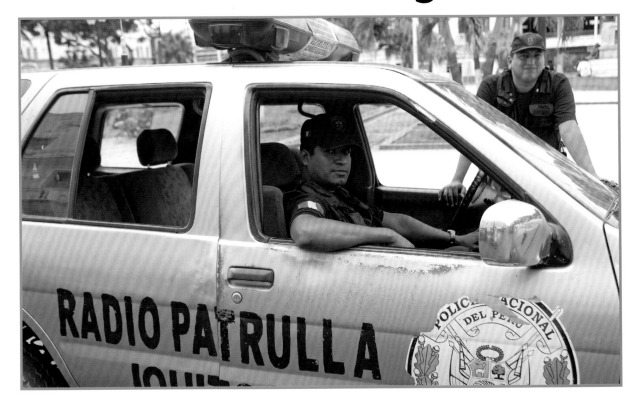

Some police officers drive cars.

Some police officers walk in
the streets.

Some police officers ride horses.

Some police officers ride bikes.

How police officers help us

Police officers help people to stay safe.

Police officers help the community.

Picture glossary

 community group of people living and working in the same area

 police station building where police officers work

 uniform special clothes that a certain group of people wear

Index

Notes for parents and teachers

This series introduces readers to the lives of different community workers, and explains some of the different jobs they perform around the world. Some of the locations featured in this book include Transylvania, Romania (page 4); London, England (page 5); Basel, Switzerland (page 11); Saskatchewan Province, Canada (page 12); Iquitos, Peru (page 16); Vincennes, France (page 19); and Tokyo, Japan (page 20).

Before reading
Explain to the children what a community is. Talk about the people who help us in the community. Tell the children they are going to learn about the work of the police. Ask the children what they think police officers do? How do they help us? Make a list of their suggestions and check it after reading the book. Did they think of everything?

After reading
• Teach the children the poem: *Officer, officer, What do you do? I help you stay safe, In all that you do.*
• Use art paper to make police officer hats and badges for the children to wear during role play activities.
• Organize a role play activity based on a mother who has lost her child while out shopping. Set up the role play area as a shop or market, with two children dressed as police officers on patrol. The mother should ask the police officers to help her find her child. Encourage the children to think of questions the police might ask: hair colour, eye colour, what was the child wearing etc.